A Rogers County Memoir
a daughter's perspective

Cindy Weever
Rogers County Press

Published by Rogers County Press
https://rogerscountymemoir.net
ISBN: 978-1-7349456-0-7

Cover and interior design by Chiwah Slater
https://awritetoknow.com

This book represents a true account of the events described herein, as called to memory by the author.

Dedicated to Gilbert Noble,
who encouraged me
in this two-year project, start to finish,
and to Dr. Murray Bennett,
who read my manuscript.

Table of Contents

The Farm

Tulsa began to encroach upon the farm, compromising the moonshine operation and causing the family to move east to Catoosa, in Rogers County, Oklahoma, where the homestead still stands today. They continued to make "whisky" illegally in this even more remote location to pay for the farm.

Bates was from the Kentucky/Tennessee area, and his family could step into the next state's jurisdiction as needed when pursued for their crimes. After they ran out of state border crossing options, probably with warrants out in both states, they moved southwest to settle in Oklahoma.

My great grandmother Adella told me she came as a girl with her family to Collinsville, Oklahoma, in the 1890s, in a covered wagon from Missouri (pronounced "Mizoura"). She gave birth to a bastard son, Russel, in 1904, prior to her marriage to Bates. Russel took the family name, and family members never again discussed his birth father, although when Bates was angry with Russell he would call him "that bastard son of yours."

All I heard about Russel was that he would tie the plow horse to a fence post and disappear into Rogers County. He undoubtedly headed along the bank of the Verdigris River into deeply wooded blackjack oaks and thick blackberry brambles, past the site where the Skelly Lodge was built in 1930, to a curve in the river where large black snakes hung in the trees. He passed this oft-repeated vanishing behavior to his son, Bob, my father.

During the large migration west known as The Great Depression, my family was so poor they barely noticed the economic downturn. The family survived by farming, ranching and hunting small game both before and after my birth in 1957.

I was told that Catoosa, an old cow town that alternated between dusty and muddy, was built in an area the Native Americans claimed was safe from tornados. As in any other old town of that time, a hotel and a post office stood at the main intersection near the Atlantic Pacific railroad. The cowhands would herd livestock down Main Street to the railyard to be loaded onto boxcars headed east to the closest Cow Palace market.

I remember going to the post office as a child, looking in the windows of the old hotel at the old-fashioned, run-down but once-posh lobby. Shortly thereafter, after a new post office opened down the street, the old post office was torn down and its mailboxes sold as keepsakes. The old hotel, which had been boarded up for some time, burned down a few years later.

Bates and Adella (also known as Delly) and her son, Russel, built a one-room home in 1918 to go with an already present sandstone chicken house. They hid the still in a densely wooded twenty acres of thick, thorny, skin-ripping wild blackberry patches only cattle could endure. I would get lost as a child in the tangled native woods, until the day a bulldozer pushed selected trees over into piles rife with small game for us.

Bates had built a barn and fishing shed, but they're gone now. As a child, I was fascinated by old, rotting fishnets my father had tied years before when he fished with an electric current that allowed him to quickly scoop up the stunned fish. That was his way of supplementing the food supply. Although quite poor, the family always had plenty to eat.

Adella had three more children with Bates, of which only two survived. Edward died at fourteen after complications with a broken limb. After my father's death, we found a suitcase full of moth-eaten wool clothing a child of his age would have worn that had sat balanced on two cross timbers in the attic above her bed for seventy years.

I heard that Hazel, the only daughter, recruited Bob to help her with insurance fraud. Bob supposedly burned down her house, another of his specialties.

One special memory I have is of Hazel's dog, Muffy, a sweet little Schipperke, repeatedly running away through the woods to our farmhouse. Not a warm person, Hazel would hit her with a newspaper. When Hazel had had enough of this back and forth with the dog, she delivered Muffy (who had had enough too), her bed, food and toys to our back door. My mother, Lois, who is a dog magnet, acquired several dogs this way. The dogs just knew they had to be with her, no matter what. She has always been The Doggie Angel.

The youngest child of Adella and Bates was Ray, who grew into an alcoholic no one but his mother wanted to associate with. Ray had no heirs. When I was in middle school, Bob bought Ray's third of the farm from him, paying for it in monthly payments. He now owned two thirds of the homestead, which was good, since it seemed he was the only one who cared about it.

This arrangement allowed Ray to keep drinking, the one thing he did well. Once when Bob was in court, on the witness stand, an attorney asked him if he could depend on Ray. He replied, "only to take another drink," eliciting a chuckle from the courtroom. I always said he was "worthless as tits on a boar."

Russel married Edna Mae. They had one son, Bobby Gene, my father, known as Bob. Edna Mae seemed to believe that Russel's father, Bob's grandfather, was one of Adella's sisters' husbands.

When they married, Edna Mae was fifteen years old. Edna said her sisters told her to marry Russel because his family always had food to eat. Edna and her sisters were so hungry they stole apples from a local orchard. When the owner caught them, they pretended to be deaf and dumb. Marrying Russel was definitely the best thing for Edna!

On May 19, 1927, Bobby Gene was born in one of the two bedrooms at the homestead. The following year, the family moved to an old, one-room shack in Collinsville, Oklahoma.

One cold, snowy night in 1929, Russel came home to a cold home, heated only by an old cook stove. He reached for a can of kerosene to build a fire to warm the cold room. Edna's yell came a second too late. Russel picked up a can of gasoline and dashed it on the fire, killing himself and others present. As the tinderbox exploded into flames, Edna broke the thin, wavy glass in the window next to her bed and climbed to safety.

Then she realized that eighteen-month-old Bob was still in the bed. She immediately climbed back into the flames through that broken window and hurried to wrap Bob in blankets. On her way back out to safety, her gown caught fire. She rolled in the snow to put out the flames. Russel lived another day. Only Edna and Bob survived that winter. Russel's father, Bates, died of stomach cancer the following year.

A widow at sixteen, Edna remained at the farm for a short time with Bob and Delly. Then she left to find a job so she could make a better life for herself and her son. She struck out on her own, hoping to send for Bob at a later date. She met and married Harold Smith, who smoked unfiltered camels and drank continuously. He was stationed in Fort Bliss, Texas, until he left to serve in WWII. An unpleasant man, Harold abruptly moved his ill-tempered, domineering mother into the El Paso apartment to prevent Edna from bringing her son from the farm to live with them. By the time Edna was able to send for Bob, he had pigs and cows to care for and wouldn't leave the farm or Delly. The feeling that she had failed him haunted Edna for the rest of her life.

Edna attended a Beauty College, which she purchased after graduating. She continued to teach at the college until she sold it and opened a salon in her El Paso home, the first home she paid for herself. The downside was that the deed had to be in a man's name, because women did not have the right to own property at that time.

The only thing likable about Harold was his writing. He wrote beautiful love letters to Edna while she was away, but upon her return he would hit her when he got drunk, which was every day. One day Harold backed her into a corner, and as she reached out to steady herself on a desk her fingers brushed against a brass statue of a dog. Without thinking, she picked up that dog and hit Harold. His glasses went flying, and the statue knocked out his false teeth. After that, he never hit her again.

Edna had no choice but to stay with Harold, as her home, purchased with her own money, was in his name. Later, after Harold and Bob had died, she moved back to Tulsa. She lived long enough to see the deadly effect of Delly's influence and the Rogers County environment had exerted on Bob's future.

The Equalizer

Delly told me a story about a white bull-dog Bob had found somewhere. He and the dog adopted one another around 1932. No one could control Bob, even when he was a small child. Delly couldn't handle him, though she had the most influence on him. He was Russel the bastard's only son, and they always maintained a close relationship. Bob roamed the county for years and knew everyone and every bit of the land like the back of his hand, just as Russel had.

The white bulldog accompanied him everywhere he went, and the two of them wouldn't go home until they got good and ready. I suppose that even then, Bob knew he needed a way to protect himself. He was a little guy, and the bulldog made a good weapon. Family and friends spoon-fed him stories of old-time gunfights and other lawless activities, and he viewed a weapon of any kind as his 'equalizer' in a fight.

One day, Delly had had enough. She told him, "the old boogeyman is gonna git yer if yer dunt start stayin closer to home." He took off the next day, as usual, disregarding what he was told. Delly quickly dressed up as the boogeyman and took out after him. The disguise must have been good, because he didn't recognize her. Nor did the bulldog, who was startled and began to growl. As soon as she caught up with them, she said in a gruff tone, "I'm tha' boogeyman tha' gits lil' boys. Git outta here now and take tha' dawg of your'n."

She told me Bob was a brave varmint and stood his ground. He told her to leave him alone or he would sic his dog on her. The dog, on cue, began inching toward her, growling, pulling his lips back to bare his teeth. She said Bob and the dog finally took off in a dead run for the house. She followed, knowing she had to beat him home without being seen. She arrived first, out of breath, and quickly stashed her disguise, not saying a word about the boogeyman.

Bob stayed home a day or two, and then ran off again to parts known only to him.

He roamed Rogers County for the rest of his life, just as his father had. In later years, while I was still living at home, the county sheriff would set up roadblocks to arrest Bob so he could question him. Bob said he would have gone to Claremore, the county seat, to speak to the sheriff, had he bothered to call. He may have been a lot of things, but he usually did what he said he would. But the sheriff found the roadblocks more dramatic and exciting.

Bob, being smarter than the sheriff, would put on his cap and jacket and disappear into the woods, down the Verdigris River. Once he told Lois, my mother, to gather his guns in a gunny sack and take them to his aunt Hazel's. Lois could not drive the guns to their destination due to the roadblock, so she dragged them through the same woods Bob had exited just minutes before. Many of the guns became scratched as they bounced off stones and one another while being dragged in the gunny sack. Hazel would hide them, because Bob had told her the sheriff would be paying us a house call in his search for guns.

The shenanigans never ended. When the sheriff tired, got bored, or ran out of overtime money, the roadblocks would go away and Bob would return home.

The War Years

Before Bob finished high school, he and Eugene, his best friend, decided to take Eugene's motorcycle to El Paso to see his "Maw," as he liked to call Edna. A little over halfway to El Paso, they passed a truck that made a left turn without signaling, almost killing them both.

World War II was raging, and they were wearing army-green khakis. The accident happened near Amarillo Army Airfield, the rescuers took them to the hospital there thinking they were in the service. Eugene had been driving and had taken the worst of the hit. The doctors didn't know if he would make it through the night. He did, but he lost one eye and walked with a limp ever after. Bob broke both legs and his jawbone and received a traumatic brain injury that would worsen as he aged.

The two spent months mending in the hospital. While they were there, someone gave Bob everything he needed to make teddy bears. I have one of the bears he made. It was given to me when I was old enough. He was made from dark gray heavy-duty, nappy fur that looked "like the cats had been sucking on it," and he had light brown button eyes. I named him Pepper. Years later, when I worked at the Tulsa Zoo, I adopted a fox terrier mixed-breed from the pound and called him Pepper. Pepper the bear is one of my favorite keepsakes, and Pepper the dog was a good friend who helped me through some difficult times.

Edna visited Bob a few times in the hospital, traveling on the greyhound bus. She paid for his hospital stay. I recently found the receipt, signed by Charley V. Newman S/Sgt., ASN 38005008, dated January 6, 1945.

Bob finished his senior year of high school at Catoosa when he was nineteen, graduating a year behind the rest of his class.

Eugene married Wanda, one of the kindest, happiest people I have ever known. She told me a story about how Bob helped her when one of her younger sons fell into a deep, empty well. She'd been beside herself, unsuccessful in her efforts to rescue him, when Bob drove by looking for Eugene. Between them, they had enough rope to pull him out of the old well. The boy was injured, so Bob drove Wanda and her son to the closest hospital. She never forgot what he had done for her. She came to visit me after my father's death to tell me her story.

Deer Hunting

Bob could not legally own a gun due to a 1950 arrest for unlawful transportation of liquor, though the charge had been reduced to transporting illegal beer. (Oklahoma liquor laws were the most backward any state could dream up. As a college student in the 1979, I had to BYOL (buy your own liquor) to take dancing. Per-drink liquor purchases didn't become an option until 1985.)

Bob kept handguns for close-range protection, and shotguns suitable to shoot through walls and doors. He hid them in the sofa cushions. He also had rifles and shotguns for hunting game—always out of season, for maximum hunter safety. He kept one behind every door.

I recall one winter when Bob and three or four buddies went deer hunting after the season had closed. They went into New Mexico to hunt and camp, to a place a native friend told them about. They took their horses in our four-horse trailer. They needed the horses to carry supplies and to get through the thick brush in the snow. They rode uphill into the forest for several days to make camp. The slopes were slick, and Bob said his horse slipped several times.

Bob's horse was one we had raised. We'd named him Blue Bunt, but we shortened it to Bunt. He was a big, raw-boned, light-colored bay gelding, and he had the roughest trot of any horse I have ever ridden. Yet he was sure-footed and calm during intense travel. He never hesitated and always cooperated, trudging up and down steep mountainous terrain. Bob's buddies, not so lucky with their horses, were amazed at how well Bunt took it all in stride. The horse was always up for any adventure. A great horse to ride, except for the trot. He was ugly but friendly, never wild or threatening. I always thought he would be a great horse for the trail or one of those long-distance races I had read about in magazines.

The hunt was quite a success, furnishing plenty of meat for the hunters' families. On the way down the mountain back to their truck, Bunt had no problem carrying a deer behind Bob's saddle, nor with the smell of the deer's spilled blood nor with its rack gigging him in the flank. He carried Bob down the slope, slipping and sliding, sometimes on his hindquarters. Less sure-footed and uncomfortable with the smell of blood, the other horses hesitated when asked to follow Bunt down the steep, slippery slopes.

At last they made it to the truck and trailer. Knowing that the truck and trailer would be searched by the local rangers, the men loaded the deer meat into the hay manger under Bunt's nose. Knowing the men had been deer hunting, the rangers inspected the entire trailer, but they never removed the horses, nor did they look under the prairie hay Bunt stood munching.

Back at the farm, the deer were hung in the barn to be butchered with the usual tools. I say "usual" because I recall Bob using a chainsaw once to cut up a steer in his shop. I always refused to enter Bob's shop while he was cutting beef. Bob's good friend was not so lucky. I think the meat is still stuck to the ceiling.

Moonshine and Chains

Long before my birth, Bob used to drive around selling his moonshine whiskey. He kept his money in a crumpled paper sack he stored under the front seat of his car. He said no one ever found it, I guess because it was in plain sight. He was a wizard at hiding money, guns, paraphernalia and himself.

During the years when he sold liquor, he learned to fight with chains. I assumed it was because he couldn't legally carry a gun. I always wondered why he never bought his guns at a gun store. He kept his guns in every corner of the house all throughout my childhood, and carried chains—not tire chains—in the car, and brass knuckles and a huge very, very sharp pocket knife in his pocket. I watched him sharpen that ominous knife to a razor's edge every week in our living room.

Walter's House

In 1960, when I was three, we lived in a small white house in Tulsa, known as Walter's house. It was a one-bedroom, with wood floors and concrete steps outside.

I slept in a crib in my parent's room. I remember my mother, Lois, but Bob always came home late, way after my bedtime. One evening, my mother and I were at home, as usual. I was in the bedroom asleep, the door slightly ajar. My mother was sitting in the living room reading a magazine when we were startled by a loud explosion. When I called for my mommy, she rushed to the side of my crib, reassured me and tell me to go back to sleep. Then she returned to her reading.

Before I could settle into sleep, my father calmly opened the front door and came in alone. I heard his and my mother's muffled voices through the closed bedroom door, though I didn't understand what they said. I returned to sleep at that point.

Bob owned a bar called The Joint, not far from our house. Since I could not pronounce the letter "j," I would substitute a "d" and ask my daddy if he was going to "The Doint" when he left mid-afternoon. The Joint burned a few weeks after the explosion, the result of an act of revenge. I gathered from my mother's whispered conversations with her best friend, Joann, that the explosion had occurred in a competitive bar in the same neighborhood. Everyone had come to the conclusion that my father had been responsible for that explosion. A few days later, the FBI came to our door to ask my mother questions, I assume, about the explosion.

To this day, I believe that was the first time my mother became truly frightened. She was not keen on their lifestyle, to say the least, and she must have felt vulnerable with a small child to care for. She never knew my father's whereabouts or what he was doing. Since Bob never shared information with her, she couldn't tell the FBI anything. Little did she know, a lifetime of such incidents awaited the two of us. Had either of us ever spoken to the authorities, there would be hell to pay.

We knew where we stood in the pecking order, and kept quiet. No amount of information could be pried out of either of us. I was warned about speaking to anyone about Bob or his activities.

You have to understand that my mother had grown up poor, in a dysfunctional, alcoholic family. She never knew what a home life should be like. In retrospect, I can understand why her father drank so much. Lois's mother, Susie, drove everyone to drink, including Lois's two older brothers. Susie constantly caused problems between Lois and her brothers and made her feel bad about herself. Later in Susie's life, she adopted a most unpleasant, hateful disposition that worsened as she aged.

Susie's second husband, Mr. Potts, was a kind old man, the type of person who would rather die than tell a lie. Not long before his death, he described to us how he watched an ugly, disfigured devil step out of Susie, laugh at him, and then jump back inside. We believed him because we knew her well and it explained a lot of things.

The Horses

Lois wanted to move out of Walter's house and leave the Tulsa area, Bob was afraid leaving so soon after the explosion and fire would make him look guilty. Three months after that incident, we left Tulsa for Sunland Park, New Mexico, with a stable of racehorses. It was there we put together our first stable.

Sunland was just across the state line from El Paso, Texas. Bob trained thoroughbred and quarter horses there in winter, and took them to Ruidoso Downs, New Mexico, every summer. He warned us once more to not speak to anyone about him or his activities, and I became good at acting dumb. Later, I would learn to adopt a poker face and not react at all.

Bob recruited me as his lookout in the stall while he worked on the racehorses. He learned from an old racehorse veterinarian how to perform many of his own veterinary jobs. He did injections, including cortisone when fluid formed and caused inflammation and heat in the horses' ankles and knees. After he worked on a horse's legs, my mother would apply a Ball solution liniment wrap every evening until race day, when they put ice boots on the horse until post time.

In the '70s, we would add dimethyl sulfoxide (diesel particulate) to the Ball solution. The DMSO would go straight into the bloodstream, taking the solution with it. Bob even gave DMSO to Delly to mix with her topical knee solutions. I tried it once on my skin and immediately began to taste onions in my mouth.

While we lived in an El Paso garage apartment, close to my kindergarten, I would sneak into the neighbor's yard to pick pomegranates. I was too shy to ask permission. They were my favorite fruit for a while, because they did not grow in Oklahoma. They liked the mild El Paso climate and so did I, most of the time. The worst of the El Paso weather was winter sandstorms. (I can still feel the sting of the sand, like needles and pins on my bare legs.)

We moved to a horse farm the following year, where I attended a poor Mexican immigrant community school in Canutillo, New Mexico. There were only two white girls, myself included, in my first grade class. During my second year of school, President Kennedy was assassinated. The school let out early so parents, most of whom were Catholic, could pick up their children. It was a turbulent time. Along with the rest of the country, I watched on television as Lee Harvey Oswald, Martin Luther King, and Robert Kennedy were assassinated. I found the emotions around Kennedy's death confusing, because Bob, a "good old boy," had not liked him. It was many years before I realized the significance of that time in history.

We lived on a horse farm surrounded by cotton fields leased to farmers and owned by Johnny and Ann Bean. We could walk down the driveway and through a patch of tall grass to the banks of the Rio Grande River, which flooded at least once every year, killing several people. I understand the fields are now planted in peppers. On the road behind the fields stood huge trees covered in mistletoe, which we easily shot out of the treetops at Christmas.

Johnny also owned the Bean Tack Supply at Sunland Park. He fixed up an old building that had once been the maid quarters, across the driveway from his house, for our small family to rent. He painted the floor gray and my mother made floral curtains for the windows. Edna, who was still in El Paso, a short drive away, bought the fabric. Wide, waist-high bookshelves divided the kitchen from the living area. Since there was only one bedroom, I slept on a cot behind the bookshelves in a corner of the kitchen.

Johnny was always good to us. Many years later, when he heard of my father's death, he would send my mother and me a check.

Edna often took my mother and me shopping. Taking pity on our poverty, she bought everything we owned, including, but not limited to, clothing, sheets, towels, dishes and my toys. My mother loved Edna more than her own mother, Susie, who refused to mind her own business and caused family problems.

We were lucky to be a long way from Tulsa. The only times I saw Delly or Susie were when I went with my father to Oklahoma to haul a load of hay, usually prairie hay or alfalfa. Hay was expensive at the racetrack, and hauling it saved money. When Bob would stop to sleep on those trips, he would push me to the floor to sleep or send me to pick up a burger at the truck stop café. Once he almost left me at a gas station!

It was at this time we met Nikki, one of Johnny's dogs. Nikki took to my mother, as dogs often did. Dogs loved my mother, and as I have said, they would move into our home just to be with her. Nikki was a black short-haired spaniel. Her bobbed tail had a small piece of liquid-filled skin on the end that had formed when her tail was cropped. It grew slowly and waved like a flag. Nikki lived with us while we were at Bean's. She became my mother's dog, but she did not care for me. I was young and annoyed her, so she would growl when I sat next to her. After my mother scolded her, Nikki decided I was okay and accepted me as family, too. She belonged to Johnny, and when we moved she stayed behind, as one would expect.

I loved living at Bean's farm. Other people lived on the farm as well. There were a number of barns behind the houses and horse pens. A large building stood between the houses and barns, a surgery center for horses. They would lead a horse to stand next to the table and strap it in while the table stood parallel to the wall. As the horse began to relax from the drugs, they would slowly lower the table into a flat position and wait for the horse to lose consciousness.

I recall sitting on the operating table, petting the horses while they were under anesthesia. The only time I could do that was when Johnny was around. Other children were present, but I do not remember who they were. Most of the surgeries had to do with lameness or flapper problems that interfered with the horse's breathing while running. I never witnessed the other surgeries, I assume because they involved too much blood or cutting. I often went into the surgery center looking for Johnny, because he was always happy and would talk to me.

Bean's place had a house trailer near the barns that they used as a leather workshop.

I would go in there to see Billy, a jockey my parents knew well, when he was there. He almost always rode our horses when they raced. Billy also did leatherwork for himself and other people. He always seemed to have a place set up in Johnny's tack shops for leatherwork. They had been friends for many years.

The Bean Farm belonged to Johnny's wife, Ann, but Johnny put it on the map as a horse farm. Ann had inherited it from her first husband, who was much older. Johnny and Ann had two sons: Jim, a few years older than me, and Joe, a little younger. We played together, but they were always getting into trouble. Sometimes they were mean to me and accused me of doing things they had done. I was young and forgiving, so I kept playing with them. I was happy then. It seemed like the best possible place to be.

I have never felt that way since.

One day after school, the bus let me off at the back gate near the mistletoe-filled trees, as usual. My mother almost always came to pick me up, but for some reason she was unable to do so that day. It was half a mile to the barns, past the cotton fields. Jim and Joe usually walked with me, but for some reason the boys were not on the bus that day, so I walked alone.

As I came up behind the barn, I heard one of the stable hands making noises to get my attention. I looked over and saw him holding something in his hands. He had his pants unzipped and was bouncing his private parts. Even at my young age I knew I wanted no part of that. I kept walking as fast as I could and never looked his way again. I went straight home to tell my mother. She told Johnny, and we never saw that man again. Johnny fired him and sent him packing.

The following winter, we moved to a trailer park rental that belonged to our jockey, Billy. I didn't like it there, but I liked the new school much better, and made new friends. I went to third grade at Zach White Elementary School, just down the street from Sunland Park, on Donovan Drive. I made friends with Kelly, the daughter of Karl, one of Billy's valets at the track. We lived there during the winter months until fifth grade. El Paso was dusty, and sandstorms became a regular event in my life at this school, as I had to walk across the large, sandy area that separated our rental from school.

Before each race, Karl, would make sure the stable colors were available for Billy to wear. Before going to the saddling paddock, each jock (jockey) had to weigh in holding his saddle. Weight could be added to the saddle if the jockey was under the required weight. If overweight, the jocks used the sweatbox to quickly reduce their weight.

Karl would take the saddle with him to the paddock to help Bob saddle the horse and add blinkers, if needed. Once the horse was saddled, Billy would come out of the jock's room to the paddock so he and Bob could talk race strategy and tell Lois how much money to bet on which horse—especially if the winner was previously arranged by the jockeys, in what was known as a "boat race."

Someone would give Billy a leg up on the saddle, and off he would go with Bob to warm up on the track as the bugle announced the horses' entrance to the turf. Bob usually rode Valentine, the old brown nag stable pony, on "parade" to the starting gates with Billy.

Some horses needed a "flipping halter" in the gate to keep them from flipping over backward and delaying the starter bell, controlled by a man known as the starter.

Our silk colors were a solid blue. Sometimes, if the silk colors were muddy from a previous race or otherwise unavailable, Billy would wear another, similar silk color that belonged to another stable. I always noticed, but I suspect I was the only one who did.

Summers in New Mexico

The summer track at Ruidoso Downs was great. The barns were made of wood, very old and painted turquoise, which I thought was beautiful.

One day on our way home we stopped by Bean's Tack Supply, which had traveled with the race meet to Ruidoso. We arrived to pick up some horse products, and I heard my Dad say, "well, there's Nikki!" She was jumping up and down at the end of a chain at the sight of my mother getting out of the car. They were so happy to see one another. Johnny told us she wouldn't eat, so he gave her to my mother. Nikki was thin, but not for long. She was part of our family from then on, and definitely my mother's dog.

At Ruidoso I rode Valentine, our old barn nag, a lazy old plug nickel horse. I would ride him to a nearby creek not far from our barn. As we approached, I could hear the water through the trees that lined the creek bank. That old horse would plod all the way from the barn to the creek. As soon as I turned him around to go back to the barn, he would take off at a gallop. I would hold on and crouch as we rode into the deep, wide drainage ditch between the barn and creek and then back up the other side. Since it rained almost every day, the ditch was sometimes flooded.

Valentine would aim for any open stall door in the barn and try to rub me off as he hurried into the stall. Most of the time I stayed on his back. I enjoyed the ride, but not the falling. If he succeeded in scraping me off his back, my mother would pick me up, help me back onto the horse and lead us away from the barn, my short legs and tennis shoe heels kicking him all the way back to the creek, and we would repeat the whole process.

The creek was a good place for trainers to stand the racehorses to take the heat out of their legs. Many horses got hot spots in their legs after a race because of old or new injuries. Racing is hard on a horse's legs. They are heavy animals, and they pound the turf hard. We normally used ice boots on the horses in their stalls, but the creek was a great substitute.

A few years later, we began spending our summers in Raton, New Mexico. The track there was called La Mesa Park, after a large mesa visible from the track. I never went to the top of that flat mountain, though I often wondered what was up there.

I would finish out the school year there, as the race meet started before my regular school let out for the summer. It rained there every single day, and you could set your watch by the daily storms—they always came between within fifteen minutes of three p.m. The showers were just enough to settle the dust, and it was rarely too warm. I much preferred the summers in Ruidoso or Raton over those we spent in Oklahoma, where the summers were hot and humid.

In the summer of 1968, after I turned nine, we lived in a house at the end by a road and across that road lay a field of huge sunflowers. One day, my mother came home in a lot of pain. She asked me to bring her some Fig Newtons from the kitchen, which I did, and then I went out to play with the neighbor girls, daughters of a jockey named Shep who lived a few doors down. I was surprised to look over and see my mother driving off with Bob. This was quite unusual for them. They would normally pick me up or say something to me before leaving.

I was more than a little worried as their absence stretched on and the hours ticked away. A succession of people I knew from the racetrack stopped by to check on me and told me to stay with the neighbor girls until Billy came to take me home. I spent that night with Billy and his wife, Bess. Billy and I traveled frequently between racetracks in his Mercedes, often stopping to wait for Lois to catch up in her old '56 Chevy pulling our two-horse trailer. Staying with Billy and his wife felt quite normal, as I knew them well. Billy was like an uncle to me. He would tease and talk to me, even tuck me in at night. I'd grown attached to Billy, as his attention filled the gap left by my father. (Bob did not know what to do with me, even when I sat on his lap. After third grade, I'd stopped trying to interact with him or get his attention).

The day following all this strange activity, Bob's mother, my grandmother Edna, showed up with Harold to stay with me at home. Lois and Bob did not come home for quite some time. Edna explained that my mother had been rushed to the hospital for a tubular pregnancy, known as ectopic, that burst, and that she had undergone emergency surgery and would have to stay in the hospital for a long time. She said they did not allow children to visit patients in the hospital, so when she went to visit I had to sit with Harold, whom I did not like because he was gruff and hateful to both Edna and me. Edna would be gone for what seemed the longest time, and I would be so grateful for a reprieve from Harold's scary behavior when she returned.

Lois had almost died, and Dr. Godding had started surgery so suddenly her scar came out crooked. He saved her life but had to remove so much tissue that she needed a blood transfusion. Lois's blood type, AB +, is quite rare, so they had to wait for the blood to arrive by helicopter at the town's small hospital.

I did not realize until much later how close my mother came to dying that day. When she came home a long time later, she filled in the details she could remember. She said she had been rushed straight to the operating table, that the nurses had been quite frightened as they careened through the hallways with her to surgery, where she vomited all those Fig Newtons back up. She said they spread all over the floor, sending the scared nurses scrambling to clean up the mess before the doctor arrived. Bob had been there with his arm under her head when the doctor finally burst through the doors. At that point, she said, she went under from the anesthesia and knew nothing until she awoke days later.

Bob stayed at the hospital for days, as he was told she might not live through the night. Had she not lived, my fate would have been sealed. With a father like Bob, I don't know how things would have gone. I was close to Edna but was always relieved to get away from Harold. How different my life and personality would have been had my mother not lived! I still cannot bear to think about it.

Bob's Career Takes Off

After Bob arrived at Sunland Park, New Mexico, the local veterinarian gave him a book and taught him what he needed to know about soreness and injury in racehorses. He learned to feel for heat and swelling in and around the ankle and knee, and the vet taught him how to palpate the leg and identify what was needed. We also came to know a medicine called phenylbutazone, commonly known as "Bute," one of a group of nonsteroidal anti-inflammatory drugs commonly used for pain relief and lameness. Between races, we would crush Bute daily to add to cooked oats for the sore horses. Bute remains popular to this day.

I do not know when exactly, but Bob learned from trial and error how to use 'hop.' Hop is medication used to enhance performance. The trick is to make sure it doesn't show up on a urine test in the test barn. He kept footlockers full of bottles, syringes, and needles just for that purpose. He was always learning and trying human and animal medications. By the time of his death, that one footlocker would morph into three plus. He mixed medications and relabeled his hop with numbers: 1, 2, and 3. He never divulged the contents to anyone, referring instead to the numbers.

Bob was a smart man and always figured out a way to make money with the horses. It was a difficult business for poor people, and impossible for them now because the wealthy always purchase the best horses.

He became well known as a trainer. If a horse could run, Bob would make it happen. As time went on, word of his talents spread and many horse owners sought him out to train for them.

We had an old thoroughbred broodmare, Nancy Pere, at the farm. As long as she was bred to a thoroughbred, she had foals that made money at the racetracks. One of her first foals was a gelding named Cindy's Jolly Jet, known around the barn as Tadpole. He would win, but he was sickly. He would catch cold easily and often had a runny nose, and my mother constantly babied him.

When we were broke, Bob could enter Tadpole in a race and make some money. One winter he took Tadpole to Nebraska. My mother and I stayed behind because I was quite young. Bob was flat broke. Discouraged, he entered Tadpole in a $5000 claiming race, something he knew better than to do. In a claiming race, any other licensed owner or trainer at that track can purchase a horse in that race for $5,000. The trick is to not drop a good horse too low in price to win, or you may lose them. We lost Tadpole that day when another stable claimed him. My mother was so upset she cried for weeks. She never cared that much again for any horse.

Your first love is always the hardest to recover from.

A World Champion

The years 1965 to 1967 were good for us. A quarter horse named Bar None Doll that Bob trained got a lot of attention. Doll's owner was Bert Coates, of Houston, Texas. During Doll's two-year-old year, her knees had not closed, meaning her bones were not mature enough to race regularly. A small mare with an enormous stride, she could have won lots of races, but she would have ended up lame for life. She won a few Futurities when she was two, but Bob saved her for her three-year-old year. He entered Doll in every big Derby available to a three-year old in 1965, and she paid off like a slot machine.

A lot of moneyed people failed to win that year, and they were not happy about Doll. Bob slept in front of her locked stall prior to each large race to prevent sabotage. When Doll was left alone her door was locked, and the one next to it too, as a decoy.

One race stands out in my mind as typical of what we were up against, as horseracing can be a cutthroat business. After her post position was drawn, the man in charge of turf operations sent the water truck to sit in front of her lane with the water running, muddying her part of the track. We sat there and watched. Billy said he could 'daylight' the field of horses leaving the starting gate, meaning he could break out so fast she would run around the mud hole without interfering with the other horses, leaving an empty "daylight" space as she pulled away from the pack.

Someone there said that was impossible to do in a field of the best three-year-old quarter horses alive. Yet all Billy had to do was show her the whip. She took off so fast we all saw the daylight as she avoided the mud hole created just for her. She kept going to win by—you got it—daylight. Keep in mind that these quarter horses run very short distances, 300, 350 or 400 yards from start to finish. Yes, she was that good.

A famous quarter horse race known as the Rainbow Derby was the BIG one. This race was at Ruidoso Downs, whereas the previous ones had taken place at La Mesa Park. Doll was a late entry, and we had to pay a $15,000 penalty. That was a lot of money in 1965. In fact, I still consider that a lot of money! Doll's owner, Bert, was reluctant to pay because he had never owned a racehorse before, let alone a champion on his first try, which is unheard of. To convince him, we divided the late penalty three ways, $5,000 each for the owner, the trainer and the jockey. She was our baby, so to speak. All of us stood to make a lot of money!

One reason these races have such large purses is that most horse owners start paying when the entrant is a foal. Many a horse owner with big plans wastes his money, as few of those horses ever qualify for the race. Bob knew it was better to just pay the penalty to get in. As history shows, winning racehorses are few and far between! Bar None Doll won the Ruidoso Rainbow Derby on August 7, 1966, running the 400 yards in 20.34 seconds. The purse was $192,320.00.

She won most of the derbies that year at Ruidoso Downs, Sunland Park and La Mesa Park. Her multiple trophies went to her owners. We kept the blue horse blankets with the derby name and year stitched onto them. That same year at La Mesa Park, Bob's silks were painted on a metal panel because he had trained "Horse of the Meet." In September of 1967, Doll was on the cover of The Quarter Racing Record, her photo showing just how small she was. She was definitely the cover girl athlete of the horse world!

The New Barn and Rogers County

We went back to the Rogers County homestead the next winter to build a new horse barn with the winnings. The new barn had eighteen stalls, in four rows of six stalls each, with huge hay lofts above the two middle rows. There were six large garage-door openings that could be rolled down in winter and a front and back door complete with door knobs for easy entry and exit.

Downtown Tulsa was being torn down, and that's where Bob got most of the twenty-four-foot two-by-twelve boards for the barn project. They are now worth a fortune, because you can no longer find anything that length. They were rare even at that time, and once we removed all the nails they were perfect for a huge barn.

Lois had hoped there would be enough

money left over to build a small home for the three of us, but that was just wishful thinking. But there was enough money left over to replace Bob's old green truck with a nice new black truck cab, and he promptly put side boards on a new, larger flatbed trailer for it.

We always took twenty to twenty-five horses to a race meet. Bob would quickly cull four or five from the twenty-some horses in the stable, consolidating the ones he knew could make us money. He would send the culled horses home in a horse van or board them in a pen near the racetrack.

He used the new black flatbed truck to haul the horses himself, pulling a four-horse trailer behind the truck. He could haul approximately eight horses in the truck. Each horse wore a rope halter, and he kept them from fighting by loading each one head to tail with the horse next to it, separated by chains, all of them facing outward over the side boards. The horses loved the fresh air.

Having hauled many of these horses before and knowing which were likely to be ornery, he loaded them in a particular order, stallions next to geldings, taking into consideration their temperaments and which mares were in heat. We were quite a sight to see on the road, with wheelbarrows, buckets, and barrels of tack on top of the cab.

We spent every winter at the farm through the rest of my grade school and high school years, in the old farmhouse Bates had built back in 1919. They finally remodeled it when I was a sophomore in college, some years after Delly had passed.

I was miserable at the farmhouse. Bob was great while in another state, but once home in Rogers County he would revert to his old ways. We never knew where he was, and my mother and I had to take care of the horses and cows all winter. We kept the horses in the barn during freezing weather to make feeding and watering them easier.

Lois and I did Bob's work while he was off wandering about the county. We cooked oats for the racehorses in a large metal garbage can with a round heating element, because cooked oats were easier for them to digest. We fed them supplements, too, Calf Manna and Jello packages for those known to suffer nosebleeds when they ran. We fed the cows hay and cubes every day, and kept an eye out when calving and foaling began. When the weather became extremely cold, we brought the mares and cows into the barn so Lois could check them at midnight. She always checked to see if a calf or foal needed to be turned or pulled during birth. If their nipples were waxy, she knew the birth would be soon. If left to struggle too long, a mother would become paralyzed and her calf or foal would die.

While Delly was still alive, we had to live with her. By then she was in a wheelchair, because her knees would not support her. I recall taking her to a doctor in Claremore when I was very young, to Radium Town.[1] His office was in one of the old brick buildings that had once been used at the height of the snake oil and healing water boom.

Lois hated being at the farm, because Delly would make remarks about the food she cooked for dinner. Delly called it slop more than once, which offended both of us. My mother worked

1   Malley, Marjorie C., "Health Spas," The Encyclopedia of Oklahoma History and Culture. Malley, Marjorie C., "Health Spas," The Encyclopedia of Oklahoma History and Culture. http://www.okhistory.org/publications/enc/entry.php?entry=HE005, accessed May 3, 2018.

all day and had to whip up dinner quickly, but in spite of that she was becoming a good cook. Delly liked Bob and me, but was jealous of my mother. I kept my head down, as Bob would not take up for my mother when he was there. I resented it until Delly's death in 1970, when life improved slightly.

Nikki, Lois's dog from Bean's horse farm, had passed a few years earlier. We had started to spend summers at the Los Alamitos, California, race meet. They raced horses all year there, but the quarter horse season was May through August. Since dogs were not allowed at the track and Nikki was getting old, we left her behind at the farm in her later years. One of those years, we returned to find she was no longer there to greet us. She had grown old and wandered off to die within a day of the last time Lois had said goodbye.

It bothered both of us a lot. Nikki had come to live with us in happier times. She was our last connection to that happiness.

Los Alamitos

We became good friends with the locals at Los Alamitos. Doll had raced there in the late 1960s, and there were many touts (people looking to bet money on a sure winner) who came around. Some were nice and became our friends. Others would follow Lois to the $50 or $100 window. High metal walls shielded the windows on both sides, and each window had a guard, but that didn't stop the touts. They would sneak up behind her to look over her shoulder to see what number she was betting. When I was with her, I stood behind her to keep these men from getting too close. My mother was short and it was easy for them to look over her shoulder. I was taller than she was, and I would stand with my back to hers and rotate with the men, looking straight at them. Then the guard usually told them to get away.

These people could bet large amounts

of money and knock down good odds. My mother would bet two or three times to keep the odds from dropping too quickly, many times placing her final bet as the horses entered the starting gate. The bell would ring as soon as she completed her wager, and no one would notice the odds board because all were focused on the race.

Prior to the Los Alamitos race meet, we would campaign at Bay Meadows in San Mateo, near San Francisco. It was there that Bob gave me money to buy a pony to ride to the starting gates. An old Indian had an Appaloosa for sale. I loved any horse with spots, so I was excited. (I have come to believe Bob planned this incident for his amusement.)

Scratch was a light brown color, spotted all over with small white hairs, his hindquarters blanketed white with light brown spots. The Indian cinched the deal by throwing a box down on the ground and telling Scratch to get in it. The horse moved his hindquarters, sidestepping close to the box. He managed, one by one, to plant both rear hooves in the box. I later learned that Scratch did the box thing on his own every time an empty cardboard box was placed near him. But left standing too long, he would fill the box with stinky green manure.

Scratch was a "stumble bum"—he stumbled in the Los Alamitos track parade more than once. I always kept a tight grip on the reins, ready to pull him up when he stumbled to avoid tumbling over his head when he went down on his knees. He had other bad habits as well: Every evening he would roll in manure, so that each morning before saddling he needed a half-bath to get the big, irregular yellow spots off.

I went before the stewards at Bay Meadows to get my license to pony when I was sixteen, so I could accompany our horse and jockey to the starting gates. I liked being a pony girl, but I didn't care much for the red-and-white-striped jackets they made us wear at Los Alamitos. We looked like a bunch of Christmas candy canes on parade. I wore my blue velvet riding helmet and blue-fringed chaps with my name in silver across the back.

One time, Scratch unseated me on the way to starting gates. We were number one, leading the field behind the outrider, Spud, who was decked out in a red vest. Scratch spooked at something in the crowd and shuffled sideways as we passed the grandstand. Our jockey, Henry, caught the reins and held them, and I did a quick remount. Being just seventeen, of course I was embarrassed.

Scratch's final insult came when I carried a bucket of water to his pen. He had his ears back at the pony next to him. As I clipped the snap on the water bucket onto the hook and eye in the stall, he bit me between my shoulder blades. I was hurting so bad I couldn't move. That bite left a butterfly scar. Needless to say, I was glad when we sold that horse, years later.

Pony girl was the only option open to me that included riding a horse. Bob always refused to let me barrel race. It wouldn't have killed my father to buy an old barrel-racing horse and set up barrels to practice on at the farm. Any decent horse would pick his feet up to avoid falling to his knees while hugging a barrel at a fast pace.

Night racing at Los Alamitos usually meant sleeping four hours after the last race at midnight, catching another four hours after lunch, and returning to work around five or six in the evening. Then, come seven in the morning, it was my job to get an early start on training and barn cleaning.

One year, when Bob was at Bay Meadows without my mother, he lived in one of the tack rooms. I heard he would gather all the flat-broke grooms and trainers who lived on the track and take them to McDonald's for dinner. He was a kind farm boy, and people liked him. He was easy for people to be around—unless you made him angry, which didn't happen often as long as he was outside of Rogers County.

During one of our final years at Bay Meadows, Bob left a "machine" hidden in the rafters of a stall. He forgot to get it before leaving for Los Alamitos. The next year it was still there, to his relief. He could hide things well! The "machine" was a battery that had been altered to shock the horse during a race. They were illegal, and jockeys had to conceal them in the sleeve of their silks, secured to their wrist with a rubber band. Horses that were too lazy to respond to the usual noises the jockey made or to the whip would frequently respond to the "machine."

During the summer meets at Los Alamitos, our horses were stabled in plywood-walled tent barns on a weeded lot. One year we noticed a strange man working for a nearby stable. He bathed the horses completely differently than a horseman would. Instead of making wide sweeps with the hair, he made jerky, short movements up and down or small circular motions with the sponge. Bob had heard that a narc had been sent into the barn area, so he went to work to find him or her. We could see into the next stall, through the cracks where the plywood walls did not quite meet. One day Bob looked through one of the many cracks and saw the guy looking back at him. The man had no chance to spy after that, because Bob made sure everyone knew who he was. We were extra careful, and he soon left.

The winter meet had fewer trainers, so we were housed in a cement barn surrounded by asphalt. There was one female jockey, her last name being Bacon, at Los Alamitos for a year or two. An old character had named her as the mount (jockey) on one of the horses he entered that day. He stopped by to see Bob and to tell us he was "makin' Bacon." Just then, he spied my mother tossing out some baloney that had gone green in the tack room refrigerator. Before she could reach the trash, he intervened and ate the baloney in a single gulp. He was slightly rotund and not well bathed, with a long mustache that food must have nested in. He wanted to make sure everyone knew he was "makin' Bacon."

The track photographer needed photos of the trainers. Bob was almost always in the top trainer standings posted in each night's racing program, but since he would never stand for a photo, the photographer asked Lois how to get his picture. She told him, "Don't let Bob see you taking the photo. As soon as the bulb flashes, run like a turkey." Later that week, he surprised all of us when he called out Bob's name. My dad looked at the camera, we saw the flash, and the photographer disappeared into the crowd. Bob was angry, but didn't see which way the photographer had gone.

Lois and I liked the idea of him being popular enough to have his picture on the front of the Racing Form, so we were proud. That photo showed up a number of times on the front page of the Form, whenever one of Bob's horses was the favorite in a race.

Little Lady Roar

One of Bob's best friends, a man called Jim, owned a mare by the name of Little Lady Roar. We had brought her with us from Oklahoma. Lady was "Distance Horse of the Meet" in 1973, when she ran 870 yards, the longest quarter horse distance race and the only one that goes around the "hook," or turn.

The following summer, when I was a junior in high school, was the last summer we raced at Los Alamitos. We finished the summer meet and returned to Oklahoma. It was the time of year when Lady would be allowed to go to pasture and rest up for the next summer.

The racetrack officials purposely waited a few months to call Bob in Oklahoma and ask if he would be interested in bringing Little Lady Roar to the winter meet. They were proposing a pre-Christmas match race, for exhibition only, paying each entrant $10,000.00. She was to race against a thoroughbred. Bob and Jim decided they would accept.

It was tough training Lady, because she had already been at pasture for two months. Bob had to bring her back into racing condition quickly if she was to be ready by race time. (I am sure the opposition knew that.) As the race day drew near, the officials asked Bob if they could substitute another thoroughbred and give $20,000 to the winner only, nothing for second. I thought that was a red flag and the wrong thing to do. For whatever reason, however, Bob agreed. Jim was angry, and the rest of us were perplexed.

Bob did not sleep in front of Lady's stall before the race to keep her safe from sabotage, as he had with Bar None Doll. The Sunday prior to the exhibition race, he was asked to speak on a local radio show. I was excited, so I listened on the barn radio that morning. Not a talkative person, Bob answered most of the questions with a "Yes Sir" or "No Sir." Then he elaborated on how hard it was to bring Lady up to a race so fast. I wish I had a copy of the recording, or a transcript, because he did well for his only time on a radio show. He would usually only speak at horse sales, from the audience, and nearly always about a particular horse.

Lady finished the match race a poor second. It is possible someone had given her a large shot of vitamin B-12, which would not hurt her but would make her sluggish. I have no way of knowing, because she was not protected the nights prior to her race. I heard that we had made a deal with a dishonest thoroughbred trainer accustomed to winning. I suspect we had been duped all along. The owners of the track gave a party the evening of the race for our opposition. They did not do the same for our stable. Wow! What a slap in the face.

When a horse wins a race, someone must accompany the horse to the test barn for a urine sample to check for illegal drugs. In this case, both horses were sent for a urine test, so I went with Lady and a groom who had agreed to help us that evening. The opposition trainer's daughter, probably ten years my senior, was there. She was rude and taunting, which left me wondering what kind of family they were. They are still in thoroughbred racing, and I see them televised at least once a year during the Triple Crown.

By 1973, life had become difficult with Bob even away from the farm. He had become more independent of his family with the passing years, and once again roamed Rogers County when he was there and had unsavory characters stopping by to see him. He cared more about his own happiness than ours. Lois still cared for the animals in winter, and when I wasn't in school I would help unload and stack bales of hay in the barn loft.

Los Alamitos had been our only reprieve from the farm, but things had begun to deteriorate with Bob. The last two race meets had not been as financially successful as before, the only money having been made through pari-mutuel wagers at those $50 and $100 windows.

Homicide

I graduated from high school in 1975. The following summer, Bob found a job on the oil pipeline being built south from Prudhoe Bay, Alaska. It was a pleasant summer because Bob was gone, making money and sending it home for my mother to deposit in the Arkansas Valley State Bank in Broken Arrow (The bank was named after the Arkansas River, which runs through the west side of Tulsa).

Bob had gotten his job because he was a "good old boy." I had heard this term all my life and was not sure what it meant until some years later. I came to understand it as white man's lingo, meaning he deserved better than others— better than women, people of color, immigrants, or anyone else they could think of to try to make less than themselves.

While Bob was away in Alaska, we had a large garden some distance from the house, behind a fence to keep livestock out. We had to pick the vegetables to give away or can for future use. An elderly local farmer, Jack, helped us frequently and gave us tips from his years of experience. Lois's mother, Susie, and her father, Carl, also drove from Catoosa almost every day to give us a hand. Later, Lois said it was a great time for her because it gave her an opportunity to get to know her father.

The older generation of Rogers County had a long-running joke about Radium Town, named for the radium water found in 1903 while drilling for oil along old, historic Highway 66. The water contained hydrogen sulfide and sulfur compounds, and was marketed by a local doctor as a miracle cure, giving Claremore a reputation as a health resort and spa.

Bob would joke to some of his friends that they were hooked on the radium water. He would tell them, "You're rushing back so you can get some more of that radium water." He would laugh, really rub it in. My mother said to me many years later, when she was visibly angered by a new, dishonest venture,

"Bob was the one who had to rush back to the radium water."

After graduation, I enrolled at Oklahoma State University. I was glad to be missing much of what was going on at the farm. I got caught up on the latest news on my monthly visits to the farm. Something was afoot every time.

I have always been extremely grateful for the education he provided me, and for his concern for my safety. In 1977, when I was twenty, attending the university in Stillwater, Bob bought a small house trailer for me to stay in, and parked it at the edge of town. He attached a short piece of gray iron tubing to the middle of the front and back doors, through which I could slide a long, narrow bar to overlap each side of the door.

I kept the doors locked every evening. The only way to open them would have been to pull the wall out. That was not likely to happen, but just in case, he bought a special shotgun for me to put under my bed, a Remington automatic with a gold trigger and the shortest legal barrel. I thought the gold trigger was a nice touch. After telling me to shoot through the door if need be, he loaded the shotgun with 00 shot. "Keep it under your bed," he instructed. I had that shotgun under my bed for four years. I was mostly afraid of Bob's enemies, of which there were many by this time. They were unlikely to be anyone I knew.

One night in September of 1978, I was already in bed when I heard a frantic knock on my front door. As I approached the front of the trailer, I heard Lois's good friend Joann and my grandmother Susie yelling for me to open the door. I quickly opened the door, puzzled at such a late visit, and asked them to come in. "Why are you guys here?" I asked. They came inside to sit down.

"We have something we need to tell you, and your mother didn't want to tell you on the phone," they said.

I asked, "Where is she?"

"She is with Bob. He shot a man today," one of them said.

"Is he okay?"

Joann said, "Who, Bob?"

"No, the man he shot."

"He's dead," Susie said.

Joann added, "The police arrested both Bob and Lois. When we left, they were both being questioned."

I asked, "Who did he kill?"

One of them replied, "Wilson."

I was stunned. I had known this might happen at some point, yet I was totally unprepared. I took it all in with a blank stare on my face, not saying much.

Joann got up. "I have to work tomorrow," she said, "so we have to get going."

I thanked them for coming, and they left. I bolted the door to go back to bed. Just to be safe, I slept on the living room couch for a few days, in case anyone wanted to kill me in my bed, which stood under a window at the end of the trailer.

The following weekend, I drove to the farm to see my parents. Bob appeared low-key. "Well, he feels bad," Lois said, "because he killed a man."

My mother filled me in on what had transpired. She said she was doing laundry and just happened to look out the window. She knew right away something wasn't right because, she went on, "Bob was circling like a

mallard duck looking for a place to land."
She did not see him shoot the man; she saw
only the confusion that followed. They called
the police, and at some point called to alert
Susie, Joann and her husband, Smitty, who
had long been one of Bob's best friends. My
mother said they had been handcuffed, taken
in for questioning, fingerprinted, and given a
paraffin test to see if either of them had fired
a gun.

Bob was out on bail because he was a permanent resident and not a flight risk. Lois
was released after it was determined that the
incident was not over jealousy in some affair
between Wilson and Lois. (That was a hilari-
ous idea, and I think she laughed, knowing
Bob would have killed her as well had that
been the case.)

The sheriff didn't know Lois at all, and un-
derestimated Bob. Bob engaged a local attorney for a short while, but decided right away
that the lawyer would sell him out. Then he
hired a well-known criminal attorney, Larry
Oliver, from Tulsa. Larry was expensive, but
he was effective. Bob put up the farm as a
property bond to make bail and began to

prepare his defense with the new criminal attorney, who told him, "We just need to create doubt."

The Trial

In September of 1978, Bob was charged with the first-degree murder of Wilson in Rogers County Court, Oklahoma. The charge seemed a little ambitious for the District Attorney, considering the situation. My father pled self-defense in court. The trial began one year after the incident, in September 1979.

I had met Wilson only once, in our kitchen while he and Bob discussed business. Lois was there, and neither of us was impressed with Wilson. Supposedly a well-known football player from California, he was the usual dishonest blowhard that came and went through the years.

His sister was in town for the trial and constantly spoke to the local press in Claremore, which is where I read about him being a football player. Wilson is such a common last name that I was never able to verify his football career.

Bob boarded horses for Wilson, and my mother had to care for them. One of the horses ran up a huge veterinary bill that was part of the boarding costs. They were in our care for what seemed like a long time, and we never received any payment.

Both Bob and Wilson had a plan, unknown to me at that time, to kill a racehorse that was insured for $10,000, a large sum of money at that time. The thought of that horrified me. Then I found out that the horse's leg was broken with a sledgehammer, and he was euthanized because that is what you must do to a horse when they break a leg.

The payoff was the $10,000 insurance check for the death of the poor horse. Bob and Wilson were co-owners of the horse, and the check was payable to my father and Bob Wilson. The disagreement began after Wilson came back to Oklahoma to settle up with Bob. The two of them went to cash the insurance check, since both had to sign.

I believe, in retrospect, that Wilson had left California to make a living. I suspect his reputation there had been so tarnished that no horse people would do business with him, so he had to find new horse country. Oklahoma fit the bill because a large number of quarter horses are born and bred there.

That was when the problem began. Bob wanted payment for boarding Wilson's horses, and half the check that was payable to both men as co-owners.

Wilson obviously thought he could bully and cheat one more person, but Bob would have none of it. His half of the horse and the huge boarding and veterinary bill amounted to a large sum of money, which he could not afford to lose. Bob refused to sign the check, making sure that Wilson knew that if he did not receive payment for board, the veterinary bill and his half of the payout, Wilson wouldn't get his half, either.

The Insurance company made out on that deal. The check was never cashed.

Bob's demand to be paid was not unreasonable. I would have done the same. My father may have had dubious ways of making money, but he always paid his bills. That quality stuck with me: Never borrow money, and always live within your budget.

Edna came from El Paso to attend her son's trial. When Larry started the jury selection, Edna began to cry. The woman sitting in front of us turned to look at me and asked, "What's wrong? Does she think the jury selection isn't fair?" I responded, "She's just upset." Just as any mother would be, seeing her son on trial for murder in the first degree.

The bank video, shown to the court, showed Bob and Wilson talking in the lobby, followed by a visible disagreement in the bank lobby when Bob refused to sign the check. Bob had had no intention of signing until Wilson agreed to give him his half of the money and pay the board bill in full. He knew he would never get any of the board money if he didn't get it that day.

Wilson snapped up the check, so Bob turned and headed for the door to return to Wilson's car. Wilson followed him to the car and they started to pull away, but as Wilson prepared to leave Broken Arrow Bob decided to jump out. He disappeared around a corner.

Joe, a good friend of Bob's, was across the street and saw Bob step out of Wilson's car but was unable to catch him or get his attention. Bob found another way home, and when he arrived at the farm he saw a man with black, frizzy hair get into a car. He squealed out so fast he left a billow of gravel and dust. This left Bob and Wilson face to face. The argument resumed and became instantly heated. Bob shot Wilson, facing him at close range. The bullet entered at the base of Wilson's neck.

The prosecuting attorney showed the jury Polaroid photos from the scene. The photos were left for viewing during the first trial break, between the judge's bench and the witness stand. Curious, I walked over to look at them. I saw different angles of the red-headed corpse lying on his back in the gray gravel driveway, in front of the chain link fence where we parked our cars. I did not linger by the photos, as Bob was still sitting on the witness stand waiting for court to resume.

I returned to my second-row seat behind Larry's assistants. Later, my mother said, "Don't look at the photos, it embarrasses your Daddy," and I responded, "Okay." I knew I had pushed the limit, but I had wanted to see those photos.

During the next break, Lois remembered the paraffin test done after their arrest. She told Larry, since she had not seen it introduced. Larry said that meant it was negative and had been purposely withheld from testimony. Larry approached the bench to tell the judge about the gunshot residue test, and the judge ordered the district attorney's office to release the information.

Larry was correct in assuming the test was negative. When that information was revealed, it changed the attitude and focus of the courtroom. Things were looking bad for the district attorney.

Bob testified that the reason he would not sign the check was for leverage to get Wilson to pay the board bill. Had Wilson intended to pay the board, he reasoned, he could have used the other half of the check to do so. Bob's mind was made up. Therefore, neither of them would get any money.

The tall man with frizzy hair was never identified. Bob did not recognize him or the vehicle he drove away from the scene. I found out, after the fact, that the man never existed, nor did his friend's testimony. He had perjured himself about seeing Bob step out of the car in Broken Arrow.

Larry Oliver had kept the best witnesses for last. Two men had willingly called his office after the incident and offered to testify regarding Wilson's prior bad acts. Each had agreed to receive a subpoena and had driven a long distance at his own expense. I did not know the men and do not recall their names, but I was quite impressed that they would offer to speak at the trial. They were more than happy to do so, especially after the horror they had endured during one of Wilson's threatening outbursts.

The first gentleman testified that he had witnessed Wilson holding a gun to another man's head. The second gave animated testimony to the fact that he was the man whose head Wilson had held a gun to and that he had thought Wilson was going to kill him. I recall the man stating that Wilson had harassed him in other ways, as well.

Toward the end of the trial, Bud, Edna's brother- in-law, stopped by the courthouse during the trial to lend his support to the family. During the last break, Bud said to me, "You always look fresh as a daisy."

As soon as Bud left, a man I had never seen came into the courthouse. In the hall, he told Lois he knew one of the jurors. The juror had sent word to Bob that he "would absolutely not convict Bob."

Larry Oliver said in his closing argument, "A man who lives by the sword will die by the sword." I thought, how true in Wilson's case! And I suspected the same would be true for Bob.

After the final summations, the case went to the jury for deliberation. I recall Bob whispering to someone that he had a book of matches and intended to start a fire if the verdict came out "guilty." I wasn't sure what he had planned, I felt sure it would mean more charges against him and more misery for Lois and me.

The jury took over an hour to come back with a verdict of "not guilty." After the judge dismissed them, Edna, Lois and I approached them as they filed out of the courtroom. Most accepted our thanks with grace, but I could tell by their faces which ones had voted guilty in the beginning. Some would not make eye contact.

After those involved in the trial had left, Bob went downstairs to the jail to speak to someone. He was gone quite a while. My mother, having learned to be patient with him , sat silent on a bench in the hallway. When Bob did not return, I became concerned. I was in my early twenties and had long been concerned for our safety, especially at times like this. Watching a family member be the defendant in a murder trial is gut wrenching because of the consequences to the family.

The thick metal door downstairs was locked, and I went downstairs and knocked on it. A man slid the small metal plate open so we could speak. It reminded me of a speakeasy, one of those private clubs for drinking and gambling during the Prohibition era. I could see that the window had bars instead of glass. I inquired, "Is Bob there?" "Yes, I think he is still here," the man said. He slid the scraping, metal plate across the window, slamming it as quickly as he had opened it.

A few minutes later Bob came strolling

out, smiling. That was a relief, for I feared he might be angry at what I had done. He would have been furious had my mother done such a thing. I was different, because I was his daughter. He was happy as he exited the jail because his ordeal was over. Mine, however, was just beginning, and seemed to have no end. We went back upstairs to get Lois so we could go home and I could return to Oklahoma State University. I had missed an entire week of classes to attend the trial.

Years later, my mother told me, "It would have been better for us if Bob had been convicted." I did not respond because I knew men had ways of controlling the wife and family from inside prison. Even though the convicted go away for a long time, they don't necessarily stop harassing you. It only ends when they die, and even then the scars and memories are haunting and the damage permanent.

Bob would have found a way to make our lives miserable, constantly demanding that Lois do this or that. Once a person is in prison, the appeal process requires a great deal of footwork . I believe our lives would have been even worse had Bob been convicted. As it was, if Lois had tried to divorce Bob he would have killed her, even from prison.

The Getaway Truck

In 1980, Oklahoma's oil and gas economy took a big nosedive. There were no jobs available in town because the downturn was so bad many oil wells had to be capped, some never to reopen. The entire oil sector economy was scarred deep and wide for several years.

During this time, Bob began to steal oil field equipment for buyers he found I know not where. To haul the equipment, he used our sun-scorched gray Chevy dually (a pickup with dual tires on rear) for a getaway truck. He equipped it with extra-heavy springs and two batteries to ensure a rapid start, and installed two gas tanks, a large front grill, and a single switch to douse all the lights. I drove it a lot because it was so safe. The two batteries were my favorite feature because they made it start like a racecar.

When we sold the farm, we left some rusty oil field equipment in the wooded pasture with grass grown over them. After Bob's death, we would give the dually to a "friend" who threatened to reveal crimes Bob had committed, revelations that could potentially cause us problems.

It was during the time of the getaway truck that I brought a boyfriend home for the weekend. After the visit, my boyfriend drove back to Oklahoma State University. The next time I went home, my mother told me, "Don't you ever bring that boy home again. Your Daddy didn't like him." His hair was too long, and he wore shorts and sandals. "He said to tell you he would take your boyfriend hunting and return without him."

I knew the drill, but the death threat surprised and concerned me. I never again brought a male friend home.

In May of 1981, Roger Wheeler, the owner of World Jai Alai (pronounced Hi Lie), was killed at the Southern Hills Country Club. Wheeler had discovered an embezzlement scheme in World Jai Alai, creating a problem for Whitey Bulger's group.[2] When I went home one weekend, I found my mother sitting at the kitchen table paying bills, extremely angry and agitated. I asked what was wrong, and she said, "Whitey Bulger's people are in town because Roger Wheeler was killed, and Bob has been talking to them. Bob thinks he's some sort of gangster."

I was more than a little shocked. The subject seemed to blow over, or at least was not brought to my attention again. Some years later, I discovered that there had been a connection between Bob and a man in Boston.

2   "Voices of Oklahoma: Roger Wheeler, John Earling" interview transcript, June 13, 2013. https://en.wikipedia.org/wiki/Roger_Wheeler_(businessman).

The Disappearance

Life on the farm had become absolutely unbearable. Threatening, and dangerous. Lois found Bob's behavior so unacceptable that she moved from the farm to Claremore. Claremore was smaller and less expensive than Tulsa, and she knew people in town. But Bob would have found her no matter where she had gone.

And find her he did.

It all started when Bob opened a bookie joint that served alcohol and offered backroom gambling. The bar was comfortable, with TVs and couches you could spend the night on, if needed. They usually served BBQ on the weekends and holidays to draw people in to eat, drink, and gamble in a back room.

Bob had loaned his partner in crime, Jerry, thirty thousand dollars to get the business started. He kept close tabs on Jerry. Since

Jerry never paid him back, one would assume his life would have been much easier without Bob hanging around.

The joint was on the edge of town on OK highway 88 to Inola. Knowing this, I found a part time job in Stillwater and continued my studies at Oklahoma State, taking an average of six hours of graduate-level classes each week. I was too depressed to begin a research project. I had some friends in Stillwater who were going to Ouray, Colorado, for the summer. That was a godsend, because I wanted to get as far away as possible.

My mother had just moved out. When she decided to move, I went to the farm to help her load her car. She had already started before I arrived. As I began helping her load the open trunk, Bob drove up in his old four-door Dodge. He stepped out of the car covered in blood, and I stood there staring, my mouth open. His three-day beard was white as snow. His hair had turned to silver prior to my birth, and the blond rinse he used was faded and stripped by strong shampoo.

No wonder Lois wanted to move out! Their relationship had deteriorated beyond repair.

I said hello, and my dad answered, "Go help your Maw." I replied, "I am helping her." He went into the house. Knowing he would not hurt her as long as I was present, I followed him in to help her explain that I was helping her load the car for her move.

Lois rented an apartment in Claremore, and I helped her carry the furniture up the stairs and set up her new place. I went to town a few times before leaving for Colorado and I was introduced to some of her new acquaintances and the lady who served her lunch behind the bar every day. Lois knew enough people in town who also knew Bob that she could keep tabs on what he was doing.

Since she couldn't take her precious dog, Muffy, given to her by Bob's Aunt Hazel a few years earlier, Lois left the dog outside with plenty of water and hoped Bob would come home to feed her and our only stallion, Piggen Pere, whom she left in the barn with a large water trough. She turned all the other horses out to pasture.

Lois would not see little Muffy again until after Bob's death.

Bob found Lois in short order and began harassing her in her apartment. I had left to work in Ouray, Colorado. Susie let me know what was happening, and shortly thereafter, my mother disappeared again. This time only Susie knew her whereabouts. I didn't want to know, for fear that Bob would press me for her location. I was glad she was beyond his reach, at least for a while.

She told me later that she had frantically loaded her car and put everything she owned except her clothing into storage, fearing that Bob would drive up and see her packing. She had begun to fear for her life after Bob had followed her in his car one day. As she waited at a railroad crossing for a train to pass, she looked in the rearview mirror and saw him step out to open the trunk. "He had been keeping his guns in the trunk," she told me. "While he was out of the car, the train passed and I hit the gas and got away before he could get back into his car." She lost him by making some quick turns.

She had previously spoken to the apartment manager and explained the situation to her. When her apartment was emptied, she left a small cactus on the windowsill, closing the drapes carefully to make sure no one could see into the apartment from any angle. It looked as though she was still living there, just not at home, giving her time to get out of town before Bob figured out she was gone.

After Lois's disappearance, I called my father every week to check on him. I called many times before I got him on the phone. Our conversations were always brief, as there wasn't much to talk about. He would ask, "How 's your car running?" And a few times, "Have you seen your Maw?" And I would reply, "The car is fine. No, I haven't seen her." Then he would ask, "Do you know where she went?" And I would reply, "No, I have no idea." Before hanging up, I would say, "I love you." I felt the need to say something meaningful because I knew he could not go on much longer in his state of mind.

The following May, I went to Oklahoma to see my father. I heard he had been staying at home and was sober, although he had never been an alcoholic or a smoker. I had never seen him drink more than three beers. I believe he always wanted to keep his wits about him to thwart danger.

He stayed at home to spend time with me while I visited. He was happy to see me, and I him. He was still in one piece, but I was falling apart emotionally. I never let most people know the extent of the upheaval in my life. I suffered from such severe depression that I had been unable to hold down a real job since I had graduated with a BS degree in Zoology in 1979. There was nothing to be done, and no way to explain how bad it had become.

Bob's birthday was the 19th of May and Father's Day was in June, so I sent two different cards at different times. I sent them early; I did not wait to bring them with me because I had a strong feeling our time was running short. I was glad to see them on top of the TV as soon as I arrived. Each card was standing up so he could see them in front of the granite clock and the statue Edna had given him of John Wayne on a horse.

After my arrival at the farm, all my old feelings came back and hit me full force. I thought it a good idea to clean out my bedroom closet, since my mother was no longer there. The back door was never locked, and I could only imagine who might walk into the house while Bob was gone.

My visit was eerie, at best. Bob was doing normal jobs around the farm and in his shop and barn. He came to the house and said, "Come go with me to check on the cows." "Okay," I agreed, and we set off in one of the old battered farm trucks. It was a typical trip to make sure all the cows were fine and to count them.

Only one thing stands out in my mind from that drive: as we drove around the pasture, it was as though Bob was looking in every direction at once. His head was on a swivel, like he was looking for someone who would also be looking for him. I spied a handgun on the seat between us and a shotgun, the barrel pointed to the floor, the stock resting on the seat, also between us. And there was another long gun in the window rack behind us.

That told me just how bad things were. I don't believe the two of us left the farm together while I was there. I felt the need to go to Susie's house every evening just before dark, but I also wanted to stay some nights at the farm with my father. Truly, I felt chills go up and down my spine at dusk. I would become frantic beyond the ability to think, for no reason. I had never felt so frightened in all my life. I am not easily frightened, but I sensed an undercurrent of violence and evil, as though I should not be there. Yet there I was.

When I heard a vehicle driving down the gravel road, I would panic until the car drew close enough for me to identify the driver. I needed to know when the car left, as well. During these panic sessions I would feel the hair on my arms and neck stand on end, like the hair on a frightened dog. When the sun got low in the sky, I would become even more frightened. At night, I wondered what might happen after dark, when I could no longer identify people. Bob had been briefing me before going outside to work, so that I would know whom to expect. I had had an ongoing fear of being shot in my bed, which I later found significant. I felt my life was in danger just by being on the farm. If someone killed Bob, I knew I would be next. I suffered from these feelings every day, multiple times a day.

The violence was palpable everywhere,

watching me, letting me know Bob's time on earth was drawing to an end. I had always been receptive to things that do not meet the eye, and I listened to those feelings.

It was not a time to argue. It was time to run.

Bob came to see Susie one evening while I was there, at my suggestion. He was very low-key as the three of us talked about different things, avoiding the elephant in the room. What could we do? Pray.

Bob invited his girlfriend, Sunny, over to meet me briefly. He told me she would return the following evening to make dinner. My first impression of her was that she had no ambition to do anything except use drugs and live off men who beat her. We talked about Edna, whom she had met when Bob went to El Paso the previous winter. I don't recall much of our conversation. All I could think about was how much Sunny looked like a younger version of my mother. It was unsettling to meet a poor substitute when he could have kept the original.

Toward the end of the week, Bob said he wanted to show me something. I followed him to his bedroom, the same room in which he had been born, where he opened the closets to show me where he had put his guns. He said, "If anything happens to me, this is where some of my guns are."

I looked into the closet, seeing nothing. He said, "Step inside and turn around." I did as I was asked and he said, "Now look up." There must have been at least twenty guns hanging on penny nails, all the way to the ceiling, all of them on the same wall as the doors, entirely out of sight to anyone looking into the closet.

"The sheriff won't see them, they won't step inside to turn around and look." He was correct. The Sheriff never found those guns, though they did confiscate many other guns kept elsewhere. I forgot about them during the fury and aftermath of Bob's death and the funeral. I remembered them a week later and rushed into Bob's bedroom closet. When I stepped inside to turn and look up, there they were, never touched during the nightmare that had taken place in my childhood home since the first time I saw them.

Sunny returned as the sun was setting on

my last evening in town. She was running late because she had stopped to pick up some groceries, and rushed to begin cooking. Bob came in to get ready for dinner. I could hear meat frying in the kitchen. I felt frantic, panicky even, as I smelled the food and she served it up on the plates. I was still standing when she and Bob sat down to eat. Sunny looked too much like my mother, sitting there next to Bob. I was not hungry. Forgetting that this was a special dinner my father had planned for me, I grabbed my purse and other belongings and headed toward the back door. I walked right past them, thinking I should leave so they could finish their dinner. Bob had a mouth full of food, but they both said, "Sit down, have some dinner with us."

I had sunk into a full panic, lost my ability to focus and think. I was in a time warp, seeing past, present and future rolled into one, passing in front of me all at once. Keen to hide my feelings, I had learned how to stay calm on the outside while inside I was in constant turmoil, never knowing when the next shoe would drop. I blurted, "I'm going to go now. I don't know what Susie has planned for us tonight. I'll stop by around eleven tomorrow morning, before I leave to catch my ride back to Colorado."

I hurried out to my car and drove back to Susie's house, in Catoosa.

It was not until much later that I realized how badly I had reacted. Bob told Susie how hurt he had been that I would not stay for dinner. I should have stayed another half hour, eaten a few bites. It broke my heart to think I had hurt him. At the time, it was all I could do to process my feelings around the unending nightmare I called my life. I had no one but Susie with whom to discuss what was happening around me, my fear and concern for Bob's life, my mother's, and my own.

The next morning, I drove to the farm in stifling heat and humidity to say goodbye. Bob was waiting for me. He heard me drive up the gravel road, and met me as I parked at the gate. I was sad to be leaving, and he was sad to see me go. In fact, I had never felt so sad. I hugged him, said "I love you" one more time. He stood there mute, looking down, incapable of hugging me. He seemed overwhelmingly sad. I feared this would be my last time to see him alive. I think he knew this, too, because once I was gone he would have to deal with the life he had been living.

When I arrived back in Ouray, Colorado, I called him to let him know I had made the trip safely. I planned to call every week, as I had done prior to my trip.

Back in Colorado, I began to worry about my mother again. How long would it take my father to find her this time? On the other hand, I knew life was getting worse for Bob. I began to doubt Susie's ability to keep a secret about her daughter's location, especially when I told her I didn't want to know. She liked to talk about everything in the utmost detail, and unlike Lois and me, she failed to understand the danger of our secrets. Perhaps this time she knew she must keep the information to herself to save her daughter. She must have been ready to explode.

The Prediction

After a loved one passes, the family usually hears other people's comments about the person from times past. Most are kind. Some can be mean, devastating even. This was the case with Susie's little detail.

In this instance, Susie was aware of one little detail that I suspect she told my mother, about which Lois requested that I not be told until sometime later. Susie did in fact wait a few months to tell me. It was a detail I would never have related to the daughter of a man who had died and left a lifetime of emotional baggage behind. My mother and I needed time to process events that would affect the rest of our lives. Yet even though we both were scarred for life and way past the normal limit, Susie had to add to our concerns.

The day she told me, we had driven to her house and were seated in the living room. Susie looked at my mother and asked, "Can

I tell her now?" Lois nodded, looking down as she usually did when she knew Susie wanted her to agree. I looked at Susie, and she began telling me about a woman with whom we were familiar.

"I went to see Rosanne before Bob died," Susie said. "She told me he was going to die." Susie's tone was animated, and she was pumping her right leg, which she had crossed over her left, looking pleased as punch with herself sitting there in her favorite turquoise chair, bursting forth with all that Roseanne had said. She continued, "Roseanne jumped up and down, she jumped up and down on her chair, saying, "He's going to die, Susie, he's going to die!" Then Susie concluded her little story with the words, "That's all I know."

I said, "Really?" and then nothing at all.

I knew the woman because she was a talented card reader. She used only a deck of playing cards to read for her clients, and she always recorded the sessions. She talked quickly about things she was seeing, usually giving names and places pertinent to her more important predictions.

I could have done without Susie's theatrics

about Roseanne. I felt Roseanne was good at what she did, because the things she said were often correct. But she always stipulated, "I can't see if it's past, present or future." I would recognize things from the past, and I always remembered the things she said for future reference. I often became aware of people and their function in my life that Roseanne had spoken to me about. Many of her predictions turned out to be accurate.

Susie later asked her daughter, "Do you want the tape made during my reading with Roseanne?" Lois responded, "Just destroy the tape. I don't need to hear that again." Susie later said she had destroyed the tape, and Mother and I believed her. We believed Roseanne, too. There was so much violence and turmoil around Bob, around all of us for that matter, that it came as no surprise that she had foretold his death.

Later, Roseanne talked about some property in Boston and Arizona. I had no idea, at the time, that I would live in Arizona for seventeen years. The Boston thing was fuzzy. I knew Bob had been in contact with a man in Boston prior to his death. I checked the city records to see if any property was registered under his name. Nothing. Perhaps there was a land purchase that had been cut short due to his death? That would have been good, since Boston was the home of Whitey Bulger's group and I already had more to deal with than I ever thought possible.

Bob's death was overshadowed by the ongoing storm of the aftermath. My mother and I were living a constant nightmare. Each day, some new crisis would arise to suck all the air out of both of us.

A Hole in the Wall

I went to bed as usual on the evening of June 10th, 1984, and slept restlessly until I awoke at one in the morning, wide awake for no apparent reason. I wandered around the apartment and finally went back to bed. I continued to sleep restlessly until morning. I wouldn't realize until later that both my mother and Edna had had a similar experience that night.

After dressing, I went outside to see what my roommates were planning for the day. A few moments later, one of them came to tell me I had a phone call. "Jim asked that you call back immediately," he said.

"Jim who?" I asked. Then I realized he meant Little Lady Roar's owner. I returned Jim's call. I asked to speak to Jim, and heard him running to the phone. His words came out in a rush: "You need to call Susie right away."

"What's wrong? Is Daddy mad at you or something?" I knew it could be any number of things, but my concern was for my mother.

Jim told me, "No, no nothing like that. Just call Susie right now." I said, "Ok, I'll call her right now." We hung up.

Before I could call Susie, the phone rang again. I answered, expecting Susie. It was Edna. Through her tears and sniffles I heard her say, "Honey, Bob is dead. Someone shot him. His body is at the morgue." I was stunned and could say nothing for a few seconds. The reality of his death came rushing over me all at once. I thought, "It has happened just as I predicted." Not a comfortable feeling.

Edna continued talking. "I spoke to Lois and she has a flight to Tulsa, arriving around six. She wants you to get a flight that will come in around the same time so Dean can pick up the two of you on one trip to the airport."

"What happened?"

"He was shot in the back while he was sleeping."

"Who did it?"

"They arrested a woman."

I was shocked, and it took me a minute to respond. "Okay, I'll make the arrangements."

She said she would cancel her ladies' hair appointments. I would see her the following day. "I love you, Cingy," she said. (That was what she usually called me. I'm not sure whether she couldn't say my name or just liked to pronounce it with a "g" instead of a "d."

"I love you, too," I said. "I'll see you tomorrow." We hung up.

As I turned to go pack, the phone rang again. This time it was Susie. I blurted out, "I just talked to Edna. She said Daddy is dead. Do you know what happened?"

Edna had stolen her thunder. "Well, the sheriff called to tell me someone shot Bob in the back while he was sleeping," she said. "He jumped up and ran through the house after the killer but fell where they found him, in front of the kitchen door where you go out to the back porch. They have a woman in custody and she's not talking. I wanted to be the one to tell you. And that's all I know." She always ended every story with "And that's all I know."

I was pleased Edna had told me. It seemed much more appropriate.

Sometime later, I learned that there were five shots fired from two guns, three killing shots that hit Bob and two strays. They were Bob's guns, the ones he had hidden in the couch, a .357-caliber pistol and a .22-caliber revolver. One bullet was never found, and the other stray had gone through the wall and lodged in the large blackjack oak tree, the one under which I had found Easter eggs in the monkey grass. Later, we would move the furniture to hide the hole in the wall.

I needed to go home. I turned to go downstairs to pack for the trip and to make an airplane reservation to Tulsa. Realizing I didn't have the airline number, I began to panic. Lucky for me, a roommate stepped in to make the reservation for a flight out of Montrose, Colorado, the closest airport. I was so flustered I could barely think. It had only been two weeks since I had seen my father.

A friend drove me to the airport in Montrose. I don't remember the flight, but I remember meeting my Uncle Dean. He looked worried and tired, his usual state. He explained that he had gone to the farm as soon as he heard Bob was dead, but that he couldn't get past the gate at the driveway because the sheriff had taken control of the property.

Dean saw one of the investigators grab something from the trunk and pocket it. "The sheriff and his men were running amok," Dean said, "stealing everything they could get their hands on from the shop." The sheriff had waited years for this opportunity. After removing pickup loads of tools, tires and anything else they wanted, he and the deputies moved to the old car bodies. They opened all the trunks with crowbars, including my mother's old Chevy, looking for money.

My first thought was that Bob had told one too many people where he kept his money, usually rolls of hundreds: in the old trunks. My second thought was that we were going to need that money. Expenses on the farm were high, and we had no way to make a living other than by selling the equipment, livestock, or guns.

My mother 's flight arrived and Dean took us straight to the farm. It was after dark by

the time we reached the last turn in the driveway and found ourselves in a bright spotlight.
Lois said, "Dean, let's Cindy and I get out
and walk in front of the car, and you follow
us. There's a very scared deputy up ahead
with an itchy trigger finger, and he has us in
the sights of a submachine gun."

The Aftermath

On day two, I saw a local newspaper article by Donna Doyle, picked up from the Tulsa World. It was about the shooting, and reported that Sunny Turner of Broken Arrow was arraigned early Monday in Rogers County District Court before Judge David Allen Box. She had been charged with first-degree murder. Bob's body was still being held by the Medical Examiner.

We would have preferred to make funeral arrangements, but the sheriff asked to speak with us. We drove to Claremore, and he told us that the Alcohol Tobacco and Firearms was getting involved in the investigation. I thought, "Oh, goody. Here comes the cavalry." Just what we needed after staring down the barrel of a submachine gun.

On day three, the ATF arrived to explain that Bob's dynamite, stored in the old Chevy, had to be detonated. That seemed reasonable. My father should not have kept it to begin with. The real kicker was, they claimed there was a tiny styrofoam ice chest with dynamite in it that had been found on the back porch. I know it didn't belong to my father and had not been there two weeks prior, and I did not believe it was his. I have always thought it was planted for sensationalism. Right away the hoorah came out in the local paper—to justify their jobs, no doubt.

We had to put plywood over all the windows facing the dynamite prior to detonation to ensure there would be no glass breakage. At the end of the day, Bob's body arrived at the funeral home and the sheriff released the property so we could finally enter our home.

There was one problem: lots of blood in the bed and kitchen. The following morning (day four), Lois, Dean and Susie went in to mop up the blood. That was a blessing, as I was not keen to be cleaning up puddles of my own father's gelled blood. Once I entered through the kitchen door, I could not prevent myself from looking down at the kitchen floor where my father had died. The linoleum was smeared and dull.

It was about this time that I realized that Muffie, my mother's little black dog, was missing. We soon learned a neighbor had picked her up the day Bob died. What had that poor little dog seen and heard? She was returned to us better than ever, to our relief. We were so thankful the neighbor had come to her rescue.

During all of the dealings with the ATF and sheriff, we were meeting with people who claimed to know what was going on. Bob had been threatened on the phone and had recorded his phone calls. We found the recorder, but no tapes. His belt was missing, too, the one he always wore.

We discovered someone who knew something but didn't want to talk to us. Claremore is a small town, and we sighted the car several times. We called the police, but never got the license number. The driver backed out of parking lots to keep us from seeing the license plate. We were attempting our own investigation, because the truth seemed elusive.

There appeared to be a lot going on and it seemed there were many who had had reason to kill Bob. There was Jerry, or Black Bart as he liked to be called. He owed Bob $30,000 for the bookie joint. Or the man Bob had gotten into a bar fight with, following which he had been due in Court on the morning of the shooting—I am sure that party would have preferred him dead. Or perhaps Sunny did kill him. She could have been forced to.

I wondered why two guns had been used.

I went into the house, and the phone rang. I answered. It was the man from Boston. He asked for Bob.

"He is out of town," I lied. He thanked me and hung up. As far as I was concerned, everyone was suspect.

The Funeral

As we continued our investigation, there was no opportunity to eat. No friends or neighbors brought any food, and after the first three days I was getting hungry. We had an apple tree with ripe green apples, and I ate those until I felt satisfied. I thought someone would bring food for us during our grief, but none did until finally Dean's wife, Betty, brought a pizza. We devoured it. Now I was good for another couple of days as we tried to make arrangements for my father's funeral. My mother jokingly told me I had lost weight in my already thin nose.

After getting possession of the farm, sleep was almost nonexistent. Late at night, people would ransack our barn and horse trailers looking for what we now know was a bale of marijuana. I know this because the bale was found twenty years later, hanging in the barn on bailing wire. Bob had hung it in a dead-end hole in the hayloft, next to the wall. I am sure he built the hole into the structure purposely just for items like the bale. The only reason it was found was because chickens were going in and out. They had a nice nest in there where hay had fallen in for the past twenty years. No one but the chickens could have found anything Bob meant to hide.

We found doors and gates left ajar every morning before the funeral until we put a locked, metal gate over the cattle guard. It didn't stop people, but they had to walk half a mile to reach the homestead.

Two friends arrived to stay with us during those harrowing nights. Mimi, my mother's good friend from Los Alamitos, came to spend several nights with us. She and I roamed the house all night every night, afraid to shut our eyes. Another friend of my father's, Cecil, came to spend one night with us, leaving on day five. I remember him sleeping on his back in the dining room, snoring loudly on the floor with one of Bob's shotguns under one hand.

We still could not sleep. My mother took one of the bedrooms, and I have no idea whether she got any sleep. Mimi and I would creep around the house to look out the windows.

We were eventually able to make funeral arrangements. I mentioned to the funeral director that we had never received the horseshoe ring my father always wore. Lucky for us, the funeral Director called the sheriff's office and proclaimed that "the dead man's family deserved to receive the ring." The ring arrived at the funeral home the next day.

The first time my mother saw Bob, her knees buckled and she nearly fainted. Dean caught her. She said, "Things could have been so different." She shed tears. After Lois and Dean left the room, I shut the doors so I could speak to my deceased father that evening. I mostly expressed that I was happy to have seen him just weeks before his death. Afterward, Dean, Lois and I went to get some dinner. I ate like a ravenous animal, and felt much calmer having spoken to my father as he lay silent.

I finally slept reasonably well, after eating, feeling safer now that the gate at the property's edge was locked. Mimi and Cecil left, and Edna came over the night before the funeral. Bob's aunt Hazel had offered her gravesite for Bob so he could be buried in the last available grave in the plot Bates had purchased in Tulsa many years prior. We happily accepted, because there was a family consensus that Bob needed to be next to his grandmother, Delly.

By day six, the day of the funeral, I decided to ask for a closed casket. Bob was beginning to smell and I was tired of dangerous antics and curiosity. I suddenly felt as though anyone who genuinely cared about my father would have viewed him at the Tulsa funeral home. Perhaps this uneasy feeling was a premonition of things to come.

Before the funeral, an angry man called. Mimi took the phone from Lois when she heard the man yelling. He was vulgar, insulting Bob in any way that came to his mind. Mimi told the man, "His wife and daughter had nothing to do with what Bob did to you. You shouldn't be calling their home. What kind of person insults the Widow and daughter of the deceased? Can't you allow them to grieve in peace?" She hung up.

The morning after the funeral, half asleep

and exhausted, I wandered out the back door in the sweltering heat and was buzzed by a small aircraft. It came straight at me, pulling up just before reaching the back patio. Unbelievable. What next? Is there no end? There was nothing to see here but a tired woman in hair rollers.

The following evening after Mimi had gone home, the phone rang. Lois answered. It was a woman from the bookie joint. She was sobbing, and very drunk. She told my mother there was a picture of Bob in his casket on the barroom bulletin board. I was devastated, on top of any already broken heart. How could a person do that? And why would anyone tell the family? The nightmare wasn't over yet.

A few days later, the man from Boston called again. This time I was truthful and told him Bob was dead. He seemed genuinely surprised and sorry, and expressed his condolence. I thanked him and hung up. I saw no reason for keeping up the "out of town" charade.

Once I'd had a few days to think, I decided the killer or killers were local. I knew we would never know the truth about everything that had transpired. Perhaps it was more than we would ever want to know.

Afterward

Sunny admitted to killing Bob. When asked why, she said, "because Bob would not let me leave." Lois's reaction was, "She could have driven away, same as I did. She had a car Bob had given her to drive."

Sunny was released on probation soon after Bob's death. I don't know whether she ever went to prison on a violation, as I never cared to know. I was angry, yes, but I felt sorry for her.

About The Author

Cindy Weever makes her home in northern San Diego County, California.

Cindy was born in Claremore, Oklahoma. She graduated from Oklahoma State in 1979 with a Bachelor of Science degree in zoology. In 1987, she began working at the Tulsa Zoo. Her lifelong love of animals led her to work on a Navy contract with the Wildlife Department at Camp Pendleton Marine Corps Base in Oceanside, California, caring for endangered species near the mouth of the Santa Margarita River. She later worked as a neurodiagnostic technician in Arizona.

She wrote this memoir to document life in Rogers County from 1900 to 1984.

www.ingramcontent.com/pod-product-compliance
Lightning Source LLC
LaVergne TN
LVHW051559080426
835510LV00020B/3049